THE PRODUCTIVITY PARADOX

NAVIGATING THE WORLD OF PRODUCTIVITY TECHNIQUES

GEORGE WATTSON

ABOUT THIS BOOK

Discover the secrets to boosting your productivity and achieving your goals with "The Productivity Paradox: Navigating the World of Productivity Techniques"

This comprehensive guide offers a deep dive into 10 of the most effective productivity methods available, including Pomodoro, GTD, Time Blocking, Mind Mapping, Kanban, 80/20 Pareto Principle, Seinfeld Method, Batch Processing, Two Minute Rule, and more.

With practical tips and insights, this book will help you find the method that works best for you and give you the tools you need to take your productivity to the next level. Whether you're looking to streamline your workday, increase your focus, or simply get more done, this book is your roadmap to success.

CONTENTS

INTRODUCTION

The Quest for Productivity

In today's fast-paced world, it's more important than ever to be productive. With so many demands on our time and energy, it can be a challenge to get everything done that we need to. That's why so many people have turned to productivity methods to help them work more effectively and get more done in less time.

In this book, we'll explore ten of the most popular and effective productivity methods. We'll take a closer look at each method, describing how it works and what makes it unique. We'll also compare the different methods, highlighting the similarities and differences between them, so that you can determine which one is right for you.

Whether you're a student, a businessperson, a stay-at-home parent, or anyone else, there's a productivity method that can help you work more efficiently and achieve your goals.

This book will provide you with the knowledge and insights you need to make an informed decision about which method to use. So, let's get started on our journey to greater productivity!

CHAPTER 1
THE POMODORO TECHNIQUE

The Pomodoro Technique is a simple and effective time management method that has been helping people boost their productivity for over three decades. Developed by Francesco Cirillo in the late 1980s, the Pomodoro Technique involves breaking work into focused intervals, or "pomodoros," each lasting 25 minutes, followed by short breaks.

The Technique is named after the Italian word for tomato, "pomodoro", as the Cirillo used a kitchen timer shaped like a tomato.

The Pomodoro Technique is based on the idea that our attention span is limited and that taking short, regular breaks can help us maintain our focus and avoid burnout. By working in focused 25-minute intervals, we can minimize distractions, increase our concentration, and get more done in less time.

One of the key reasons the Pomodoro Technique works is that it helps us overcome procrastination and get started on tasks that we might otherwise put off.

By setting a timer for 25 minutes and focusing solely on the task at hand, we eliminate distractions and distractions are reduced, allowing us to make significant progress in a short amount of time.

Another reason the Pomodoro Technique works is that it helps us avoid burnout. By taking regular breaks, we give our brains a chance to rest and recharge, which can help us maintain our focus and energy levels throughout the day.

Using the Pomodoro Technique is simple and straightforward. To get started, you'll need a timer and a task list.

Here's how it works:

1. Choose a task to work on: Look at your task list and choose a task that you want to focus on.
2. Set the timer for 25 minutes: This is your "pomodoro."
3. Work on the task: Focus solely on the task at hand and eliminate all distractions.
4. Take a short break: When the timer goes off, take a five-minute break.
5. Repeat the process: Start another pomodoro, focusing on the next task on your list.
6. Take a longer break: After every four pomodoros, take a longer break of 15-30 minutes.

The Pomodoro Technique is flexible and can be adapted to suit individual needs and preferences. For example, you can adjust the length of the pomodoros and breaks to suit your needs. If you find that 25 minutes is too short, you can try working for 30 minutes or longer. If you find that you need longer breaks, you can extend the length of your breaks.

To get the most out of the Pomodoro Technique, it's important to be consistent and to stick with it. The more you use the technique, the more you'll find that it becomes a habit and that you're able to get more done in less time.

The Pomodoro Technique is a simple and effective time management method that can help you boost your productivity by reducing distractions, increasing focus, and avoiding burnout.

Whether you're a student, a businessperson, or anyone else, the Pomodoro Technique can help you work more efficiently and achieve your goals. So, give it a try and see for yourself how it can help you boost your productivity!

CHAPTER 2
GETTING THINGS DONE (GTD)

The GTD (Getting Things Done) method is a comprehensive productivity system that was developed by David Allen in the early 2000s.

Getting Things Done s based on the idea that by getting all of your tasks, thoughts, and ideas out of your head and onto paper, you can free up your mind to focus on the tasks at hand and increase your productivity.

At its core, the GTD method involves four basic steps: capturing, organizing, doing, and reviewing. By following these steps, you can create a system for getting things done that is simple, effective, and scalable.

Step 1 - Capturing

This is the process of capturing all of your tasks, thoughts, and ideas in a trusted system, without trying to analyze or process them. This could be a notebook, a task manager, or a voice recording device.

The capture step in the GTD method is crucial in clearing your mind because it provides a way to gather all the thoughts, tasks, and projects that are floating around in your head into one central place

By doing this, you are freeing up mental space and reducing the stress of trying to remember everything. The capture step allows you to create a comprehensive list of all the things you need to get done, so you can prioritize, categorize, and schedule your tasks effectively.

This step helps you to declutter your mind and focus on the tasks at hand, which in turn can increase your productivity and overall well-being. By putting everything down on paper or in a digital tool, you can trust that you won't forget anything important and can rest assured that you have a plan in place to tackle all your tasks in a systematic and organized manner.

Step 2 - Organizing

Next, start by breaking down complex projects into smaller, more manageable tasks, so that you can see at a glance what needs to be done. In this step, you will also group all of these tasks by context - the tools, resources, or environment you will need to complete them.

By grouping tasks into contexts, you can focus on completing the tasks that are relevant to your current situation and not be overwhelmed by looking at a long list of tasks that you can't complete in your current location or with your current resources.

For example, if you're at the office, you can focus on tasks that can be completed there, such as responding to emails, attending meetings, and completing work-related projects. By using GTD, you can work more efficiently and effectively, and avoid the stress and frustration of feeling like you're never making progress on your goals.

Step 3 - Doing

The "Cranking Widgets" step is the final step in the GTD method and is where you actually complete the tasks you have organized and prioritized in the previous steps.

The key benefit of the GTD method is that by getting all of your tasks and ideas out of your head and into a trusted system, so that you can free up your mind to fully focus on each task.

To implement the GTD method, you'll need a few tools, such as a notebook, a digital note-taking app, or a task management tool. You'll also need to be willing to invest some time and effort into setting up your system and getting into the habit of using it.

Step 4 - Reviewing

The weekly review step in GTD (Getting Things Done) is an important part of the process, and it helps you to place your trust in the system and be worried that you're forgetting something or that it has got lost in the system.

The review step involves taking some time to regularly go through your lists, projects, and goals, and evaluate your progress.

By reviewing your system regularly, you can ensure that everything is on track, and that nothing has been missed or forgotten.

The review also gives you an opportunity to adjust your priorities, and make any necessary changes to your plan. By having a consistent review process, you can gain confidence in your ability to remember everything, and you can free up mental space that would otherwise be occupied by worry.

Here are a few tips for implementing Getting Things Done:

1. **Start small:** When implementing the GTD method, it's best to start with small and manageable steps. For example, begin by clearing your bran and creating a list of all the tasks you need to do and then work on organizing them into actionable tasks and contexts. This will give you a good foundation for moving forward with the system.

2. **Use a trusted tool:** The GTD method requires you to capture all the tasks and information in one place. To do this effectively, you need a trusted tool that works for you. This can be a physical notebook, a digital task manager, or a combination of both. Find what works for you and stick with it.

3. **Set aside regular review time:** Setting aside regular time for this step will help you stay focused and on top of your responsibilities. Make sure to schedule this time into your calendar and stick to it as much as possible.

CHAPTER 3
TIME BLOCKING

Time blocking is a productivity method that involves dividing your day into specific blocks of time and dedicating each block to a specific task or activity.

The idea behind time blocking is that by giving each task a designated time slot, you can increase focus and productivity, and avoid the distractions and interruptions that can derail your day.

One of the benefits of time blocking is that it helps you to prioritize your tasks. By allocating specific blocks of time to your most important tasks, you ensure that you are using your time effectively and making progress towards your goals.

This can be especially helpful for those who struggle with procrastination or find it difficult to stay focused. By alternating blocks of focused work with blocks of rest or relaxation, you can avoid burnout and maintain your energy levels throughout the day.

To get started with time blocking, it is important to have a clear understanding of what you want to achieve and what your priorities are. This can involve setting clear goals, creating a to-do list, and identifying the most important tasks that you need to complete each day.

Once you have a clear understanding of your priorities, you can start to divide your day into specific blocks of time. This may involve using a schedule or calendar to map out your day, or using a timer to help you stay on track.

It is important to be flexible and adjust your time blocks as needed, based on your schedule, energy levels, and workload. For example, if you have a meeting that runs longer than expected, you may need to adjust your time blocks to accommodate the additional time.

One of the key principles of time blocking is to avoid multitasking. Instead of trying to do multiple things at once, you focus on one task at a time and give it your full attention. This can help you to avoid distractions, increase focus, and improve the quality of your work.

Another important principle of time blocking is to include breaks and rest periods. By taking regular breaks and stepping away from your work, you can recharge your batteries and avoid burnout. This can involve taking a short walk, meditating, or simply taking a few deep breaths.

By dedicating specific blocks of time to each task or activity, you can improve your focus and avoid distractions, and create a more structured and effective schedule. Whether you are a busy professional, a student, or simply someone looking to boost your productivity, time blocking is a useful tool that can help you achieve your goals and make the most of your time.

Tips for getting started with time blocking:

1. Determine Your Priorities

The first step in implementing the time blocking method is to determine your priorities and focus areas. Take some time to reflect on what tasks and activities are most important to you and what you need to achieve. Consider your short-term and long-term goals, and identify which activities are crucial for reaching these goals.

2. Plan Your Schedule

Once you have a clear understanding of your priorities, it's time to plan your schedule. This can be done by using a calendar, a whiteboard, or with the help of app like Calendly.

Divide your day into blocks of time, and assign each block to a specific task or activity. Make sure you allocate enough time for each task and remember to schedule some time for breaks and relaxation.

3. Stick to Your Schedule

Perhaps the most important step in implementing time blocking is to stick to your schedule.

Avoid distractions and stay focused on your tasks. If you find that you're running out of time, you can always adjust your schedule or reassign tasks to another block of time.

The key is to be flexible, but also to stay committed to following your plan. The more you use the time blocking method, the more natural it will become and the more productive you'll be.

CHAPTER 4
THE EISENHOWER MATRIX

The Eisenhower Matrix was named after former U.S. President Dwight D. Eisenhower and is said to be based on his management style and priorities.

The matrix was created to help organize and prioritize tasks based on their urgency and importance, which is similar to how President Eisenhower managed his responsibilities.

The matrix is based on the idea that tasks can be divided into four categories:

- urgent and important
- important but not urgent
- urgent but not important
- not urgent or important

By classifying tasks into these categories, you can gain a clearer understanding of what tasks are truly important and should be given priority, and what tasks can be deferred or delegated.

The first category, urgent and important, includes tasks that are time-sensitive and require immediate attention. These tasks may include deadlines, crisis situations, or important meetings. Tasks in this category should be given top priority and completed as soon as possible.

The second category, important but not urgent, includes tasks that are important but don't have a pressing deadline. These tasks may include long-term goals, personal development, or relationships. Tasks in this category should also be given priority, but may not require immediate attention.

The third category, urgent but not important, includes tasks that are time-sensitive but don't have a significant impact on your life or work. These tasks may include low-priority emails, interruptions, or minor errands. Tasks in this category can often be deferred or delegated to someone else.

The fourth category, not urgent or important, includes tasks that are neither time-sensitive nor impactful. These tasks may include distractions, time-wasters, or low-priority tasks. Tasks in this category should be avoided or eliminated if possible.

To get started with the Eisenhower Matrix:

1. **Assess Your Tasks**: Begin by listing all the tasks you need to complete and categorize them based on their urgency and importance.

2. **Prioritize Your Tasks**: Using the Eisenhower Matrix, place each task in one of four categories: Urgent and Important, Important but Not Urgent, Urgent but Not Important, and Not Urgent or Important.

3. **Create an Action Plan**: Based on the priorities you've established, create a to-do list for each day or week. Make sure you allocate your time and energy to the most important and urgent tasks first, while keeping in mind the importance of work-life balance. Finally, stick to your plan and be flexible if necessary. You may need to adjust your plan as your priorities change or new tasks arise.

In addition to categorizing and prioritizing tasks, it is also important to maintain a healthy work-life balance. This can involve taking regular breaks, setting boundaries, and making time for self-care and relaxation.

The Eisenhower Matrix is a powerful tool for boosting productivity and prioritizing tasks. By categorizing tasks into the four categories and prioritizing them accordingly, you can gain a clearer understanding of what tasks are truly important and make the most of your time.

Whether you are a busy professional, a student, or simply someone looking to improve your productivity, the Eisenhower Matrix can help you achieve your goals and make the most of your time.

CHAPTER 5
MIND MAPPING

Mind Mapping is a creativity and productivity technique developed by Tony Buzan, a British psychologist and author, in the late 1960s. It is a powerful tool for organizing and clarifying thoughts, ideas, and information.

Mind Mapping involves creating a visual representation of information, such as a diagram or a flowchart, to help you understand and remember information more effectively. Mind mapping can be used to boost productivity in a variety of ways, from organizing your thoughts and planning projects to improving your memory and problem-solving skills.

By visually representing information, you can gain a better understanding of the relationships between different ideas, prioritize information, improve your memory, and problem-solving skills. Whether you are a busy professional, a student, or simply someone looking to improve your productivity, mind mapping can help you achieve your goals and make the most of your time.

The first step in using mind mapping to boost productivity is to gather all of the information and ideas related to a particular task or project. This can include notes, ideas, to-do lists, and any other relevant information.

Next, create a central idea or concept in the center of a piece of paper or a digital canvas. This central idea represents the main topic or theme of the mind map. From this central idea, draw branches or lines to represent related ideas, subtopics, or sub-ideas.

One of the key benefits of mind mapping is that it allows you to see information in a new and different way. By visually organizing information, you can gain a better understanding of the relationships between different ideas and see connections that may not have been apparent before.

Mind mapping can help you to prioritize information. When creating a mind map, you can highlight the most important ideas or tasks, making it easier to focus on what is truly important.

This technique can also be used to improve your memory. By visually representing information, you can create a mental image that is easier to recall than written information. This can be especially helpful when studying or preparing for exams.

Mind mapping can also be used to improve your problem-solving skills. When faced with a complex problem, mind mapping can help you break it down into smaller, more manageable parts and see the problem in a new and different way. This can help you to find creative solutions and come up with new ideas.

To get the most out of mind mapping, it is important to be creative and have fun with the process. Experiment with different colors, images, and symbols to help you understand and remember information better.

Another helpful tip is to keep your mind map simple and clear. Avoid adding too much information to a single mind map, as this can make it difficult to understand and remember. Instead, create separate mind maps for different topics or projects.

Finally, make sure to review and update your mind maps regularly. This can help you to stay on track, keep your information up-to-date, and continue to improve your productivity.

CHAPTER 6
KANBAN

Kanban is a visual system for managing and organizing work, originally developed for use in manufacturing but now widely used in a variety of industries and settings, including software development, healthcare, and education.

The key principle behind Kanban is to make work visible, so that everyone involved in a project or process can see what needs to be done, who is responsible for each task, and when it is due.

Kanban is a flexible and adaptable system that can be customized to meet the needs of any team or organization. It is based on the idea of a "kanban board," which is a physical or digital board that displays the different stages of a process, such as "to do," "in progress," and "done." Tasks are represented by cards or sometimes sticky notes, which are moved from left to right on the board as they are completed.

One of the key benefits of using Kanban is that it helps to reduce waste and increase efficiency by making it clear what needs to be done, who is responsible for each task, and when it is due. This makes it easier to manage work and avoid delays and misunderstandings.

Kanban also helps to improve communication and collaboration by making work visible to everyone involved. Teams can see what others are working on and can easily provide feedback and support. This can lead to better decision-making and increased motivation, as everyone feels more connected to the work and can see the impact of their efforts.

Another key benefit of Kanban is that it helps to manage and reduce the amount of work in progress. By limiting the number of tasks that can be in progress at any one time, teams can avoid multitasking and focus on completing tasks one at a time, which can increase productivity and quality.

To get started with Kanban, you will need to choose a kanban board and decide how you want to represent your tasks and processes. There are many different types of kanban boards to choose from, including physical boards, digital boards, and software-based boards. Once you have chosen your board, you can start creating cards for each task and move them through the different stages of your process.

It is also important to set clear rules and guidelines for your Kanban system. For example, you may want to set limits on the number of tasks that can be in progress at any one time, or specify how long tasks should take to complete. You may also want to establish a regular review and feedback process, to ensure that your Kanban system is working effectively.

A critical part of using Kanban is to regularly review and update your system. This helps you to identify areas for improvement and make changes as needed. For example, you may want to adjust the number of tasks that can be in progress, or add new stages to your process to better reflect the way you work.

Kanban is a powerful tool for managing and organizing work, and can be used to boost productivity in a variety of industries and settings.

By making work visible, reducing waste, improving communication and collaboration, and managing work in progress, Kanban can help teams to work more efficiently and effectively, and achieve their goals. Whether you are a busy professional, a team leader, or simply someone looking to improve your productivity, Kanban can help you to get more done and make the most of your time.

CHAPTER 7
THE TWO MINUTE RULE

The Two Minute Rule is a simple yet effective productivity method that helps you prioritize and manage your tasks more efficiently. The rule states that if a task can be completed in two minutes or less, do it now, rather than putting it off until later.

This approach is based on the idea that many small tasks, if left undone, can quickly pile up and create a sense of overwhelm, making it difficult to focus on more important tasks. By taking care of small tasks as soon as they arise, you can keep your to-do list manageable and free up mental space for more complex and important tasks.

The idea behind this rule is that even if a task seems small or insignificant, getting started on it right away can prevent it from becoming a bigger, more overwhelming task down the line.

By taking care of the two-minute tasks immediately, you save time and mental energy that would otherwise be spent on tracking the task in a system like GTD or creating a kanban card. Additionally, starting and completing small tasks can give a sense of accomplishment and help build momentum to tackle larger tasks.

To implement the Two Minute Rule in your own life, simply follow these steps:

1. **Identify small tasks**: The first step is to identify tasks that can be completed in two minutes or less. These tasks can include things like responding to an email, making a quick phone call, or filing a document.
2. **Do it now**: If a task can be completed in two minutes or less, do it immediately, rather than putting it off for later. This helps you avoid the tendency to procrastinate and ensures that small tasks don't pile up and become a burden.
3. **Prioritize**: When a task can't be completed in two minutes or less, prioritize it in your GTD or Kanban system. Use the Two Minute Rule to ensure that small tasks don't distract you from more important tasks.
4. **Refine your process**: Regularly evaluate your use of the Two Minute Rule to see if you are using it effectively. Consider adjusting the rule to fit your needs and preferences.

By using the Two Minute Rule in conjunction with other productivity methods, you can create a system that works for you and helps you stay focused, productive, and on top of your to-do list. By taking care of small tasks as soon as they arise, you can reduce the sense of over-whelm, free up mental space, and be better prepared to tackle more important tasks.

CHAPTER 8

THE 80/20 RULE (PARETO PRINCIPLE)

This principle was first described by Italian economist Vilfredo Pareto in the late 19th century and has since been widely applied to a variety of fields, including business, economics, and personal productivity.

The key idea behind the 80/20 principle is that in many situations, a small number of factors account for the majority of results. This can be seen in many different areas, such as business, where a small number of customers generate the majority of revenue, or in personal productivity, where a small number of tasks generate the majority of results.

By identifying the 20% of tasks or activities that generate the majority of results, you can prioritize your time and resources more effectively, and achieve more with less effort.

By focusing on the most important tasks and activities, you can eliminate or reduce the time and resources you spend on low-impact activities, freeing up time and resources to be used more effectively.

To leverage the 80/20 principle to boost productivity, there are a few key steps you can take:

1. **Identify the 20%:** Find which tasks or activities that generate the majority of results. This can be done by keeping track of your activities and tasks for a week or two, and then reviewing the data to see which activities generate the most results.
2. **Prioritize** the 20%: Once you have identified the 20% of tasks or activities that generate the majority of results, you can prioritize them. This means focusing your time and resources on these tasks and activities.
3. **Eliminate waste:** The next step is to eliminate waste, by identifying and reducing the time and resources you spend on low-impact activities. This may mean delegating tasks, automating repetitive tasks, or simply cutting back on low-impact activities.
4. **Review and refine:** The 80/20 principle is not a one-time process, but an ongoing cycle of review and refinement. You should regularly review your approach and make changes as needed, to ensure that you are getting the most from your time and resources.

The 80/20 Pareto Principle is a powerful tool for boosting productivity. By focusing on the 20% of tasks or activities that generate the majority of results, individuals and organizations can achieve more with less effort, and eliminate waste.

Whether you are a busy professional, a team leader, or simply someone looking to improve your productivity, the 80/20 principle can help you to get more done and make the most of your precious time.

CHAPTER 9
THE SEINFELD METHOD

The Seinfeld Method, also known as the "Don't Break the Chain" method, is a simple but effective productivity technique named after comedian Jerry Seinfeld.

It can be used by anyone looking to improve their productivity and develop habits. This method is particularly useful for individuals who struggle with consistency and need a simple and visual way to track their progress.

It's a great tool for people who are looking to make a change in their life, whether that's learning a new skill, developing a healthy habit, or accomplishing a big goal. The Seinfeld Method can be used by individuals from all walks of life, including entrepreneurs, students, homemakers, and anyone looking to be more productive and efficient in their daily routines.

The idea behind this method is to develop a daily habit by performing a small task each day and then marking it on a calendar. Over time, the idea is to build up a chain of completed tasks, which creates a sense of momentum and helps you maintain your motivation.

The Seinfeld Method is a great way to develop new habits, overcome procrastination, and increase productivity. By focusing on small, manageable tasks that can be done daily, you can make steady progress towards your goals and build a strong sense of accomplishment over time.

Here's how to use the Seinfeld Method to boost your productivity:

1. **Identify a task**: The first step is to identify a task that you want to turn into a daily habit. This could be anything from writing for 30 minutes every day to meditating for 10 minutes. The key is to choose a task that is small, manageable, and can be done every day.
2. **Get a calendar**: Get a physical calendar that you can use to mark your progress. This could be a wall calendar, a desk calendar, or even a simple notebook. The key is to have a physical representation of your progress.
3. **Mark your progress**: Each day that you complete your task, mark it on your calendar with a big X. The idea is to build a chain of Xs, which will give you a visual representation of your progress.
4. **Make it a non-negotiable**: The Seinfeld Method works best when you make your daily task a non-negotiable part of your day. This means that you should make time for it, no matter what, and avoid breaking the chain of Xs.

5. **Celebrate your successes**: Finally, it's important to celebrate your successes along the way. This could mean acknowledging your progress with a simple "good job" or by rewarding yourself in some way, such as treating yourself to a movie or a special meal.

The Seinfeld Method can be powerful in helping you to overcome procrastination. By focusing on a small, manageable task, you can build momentum and maintain your motivation over time. This can be particularly helpful when you are starting out on a new habit or working on a long-term goal, as it can be difficult to stay motivated in the early stages.

Making your daily task a non-negotiable part of your day trains your mind to develop new habits and patterns of behavior. This can be incredibly powerful, as it helps you to build new behavioral habits and increase your productivity over time.

Whether you are working on a long-term goal or simply looking for a way to get more done each day, the Seinfeld Method can help you to make steady progress and build a strong sense of accomplishment along the way.

CHAPTER 10
BATCH PROCESSING

Batch processing is a productivity technique that involves grouping similar tasks together and completing them in a batch.

The goal of batch processing is to minimize the time and effort spent on transition between tasks, and increase focus and efficiency. The technique has been widely adopted in many industries and has been proven to help individuals and teams achieve better results in less time.

The basic idea behind batch processing is to work on similar tasks in groups, rather than jumping back and forth between different types of tasks.

For example, instead of answering emails, making phone calls, and doing paperwork throughout the day, one could dedicate a specific block of time to answering emails, another block of time to making phone calls, and another block of time to doing paperwork. This allows the individual to get into a state of flow, where they can focus on the task at hand and not get interrupted by other distractions.

One of the key benefits of batch processing is that it helps minimize the time and energy spent on task switching. Task switching has been shown to decrease productivity and creativity, as the brain takes time to adjust to the new task and get into a state of flow. By grouping similar tasks together, the individual can reduce the amount of time and effort spent on task switching, allowing them to work more efficiently and effectively.

By dedicating specific blocks of time to specific tasks, you can eliminate distractions and stay focused on the task at hand. This leads to higher levels of engagement, creativity, and productivity.

Batch processing can be applied to a wide range of tasks, including administrative tasks, creative tasks, and even personal tasks. For example, one could dedicate a specific block of time to checking and answering emails, another block of time to doing household chores, and another block of time to exercise. By grouping similar tasks together, the individual can create a more efficient and effective system for getting things done.

Here are three steps to get started with batch processing as a productivity booster:

1. **Identify tasks**: Take a look at your daily tasks and see which ones can be grouped together to save time. For example, you could check your email, respond to messages, and schedule appointments all in one sitting, instead of

checking your email multiple times throughout the day.

2. **Create a schedule**: Once you've identified the tasks that can be done in batches, create a schedule for when you will complete these tasks. This can be done daily, weekly, or monthly, depending on the frequency of the tasks.

3. **Stick to the schedule**: As with all the methods in this book, the key to success is sticking to the plan. Set aside dedicated time for batch processing and avoid interruptions during this time so you can focus on getting your tasks done efficiently.

By following these three steps, you can use batch processing to maximize your productivity, reduce distractions, and free up more time for the things that matter most to you.

CHAPTER 11
LIVE YOUR BEST LIFE

When it comes to productivity, it can be easy to get caught up in the pursuit of getting more done and being more efficient. While this is a noble goal, it is also important to remember that there is more to life than just work. That's why it is so important to strive for work-life balance - to ensure that we are making the most of both our professional and personal lives.

One of the great benefits of using productivity methods is that they can help you get more done in less time, freeing up time for the things you love. By streamlining your tasks, prioritizing your time, and reducing distractions, you can make the most of every moment, both at work and at home.

One of the keys to achieving work-life balance is to set realistic expectations for yourself. This means being honest about the amount of time you can realistically dedicate to work, and ensuring that you are not sacrificing your personal life in the pursuit of productivity. At the same time, it also means being realistic about your personal life, and making sure that you are making time for the things that matter most to you.

Another critical component of successful work-life balance is setting appropriate boundaries. This means making a conscious effort to separate your work and personal lives, so that you can fully focus on each. This can involve setting specific times during the day to check your email or work on projects, as well as establishing clear lines between work and personal time, such as turning off your phone after work hours.

By balancing work and life, you can live your best life. When you are more productive, you are able to get more done in less time, freeing up time for the things you love. Whether it's spending time with loved ones, pursuing hobbies, or simply relaxing, work-life balance gives you the time and energy to live life to the fullest.

Productivity not only affects your work life but can also have a significant impact on mental health and overall life expectancy. Having a productive day and feeling like you are accomplishing your goals can lead to an increase in self-esteem and a more positive outlook on life.

So, as you work to boost your productivity and achieve your goals, remember to prioritize work-life balance. By balancing your professional and personal lives, you can ensure that you are living your best life, filled with happiness, joy, and fulfillment.

CHAPTER 12
CHOOSING WHAT WORKS FOR YOU

Productivity is a highly personal and individual pursuit. What works for one person may not work for another, so it's important to try different methods and find what works best for you. The methods covered in this book are all effective for different people in different situations.

When it comes to productivity, there is no one-size-fits-all approach. Different methods work better for different types of people and personalities. In this chapter, we will explore each of the ten productivity methods discussed in previous chapters and describe which type of person each method may be best suited for.

The Pomodoro Technique is great for those who are easily distracted or have trouble focusing for long periods of time. It's also ideal for people who enjoy structure and routine, as it involves breaking work down into manageable 25-minute chunks.

Getting Things Done (GTD) is best for individuals who are constantly bombarded with tasks and responsibilities, and who need a comprehensive system for organizing and prioritizing their workload. It's also ideal for people who enjoy being proactive and taking control of their lives.

Time Blocking is ideal for people who like to have a clear sense of what they need to accomplish each day, and who enjoy having a rigid schedule. It's also great for those who have trouble sticking to a plan or who struggle to stay focused.

The Eisenhower Matrix is perfect for those who are strategic thinkers and who enjoy prioritizing tasks based on urgency and importance. It's also ideal for individuals who enjoy making decisions and taking control of their workload.

Mind Mapping is best for creative and visual individuals, who enjoy brainstorming and exploring new ideas. It's also ideal for those who are easily overwhelmed by large amounts of information and need a way to break it down into manageable chunks.

Kanban is great if you enjoy using visual aids to track their progress and stay organized. It's also ideal for individuals who like to take a hands-on approach to productivity, and who enjoy experimenting with different tools and systems.

The Two Minute Rule is a simple and effective productivity tool that can benefit individuals who struggle with procrastination and managing their workload efficiently.

The 80/20 (Pareto) Principle is best for individuals who are results-driven and who enjoy focusing on the most impactful tasks. It's also ideal for those who have a tendency to become bogged down by minor details, and who need a way to focus on what truly matters.

The Seinfeld Method is ideal for individuals who enjoy establishing and maintaining habits, and who are motivated by positive reinforcement. It's also great for those who struggle to stay focused and need a way to track their progress.

Batch Processing is well-suited for individuals who enjoy working in large blocks of time, and who need to avoid distractions and interruptions in order to get things done. It's also great for those who enjoy working in a focused and uninterrupted environment.

Ultimately, the best productivity method for you will depend on your personal preferences, work style, and lifestyle. Take some time to experiment with each method and see what works best for you. With the right approach, you can increase your productivity, focus, and overall well-being.

Creating a customized plan is key to maximizing the benefits of productivity methods. By taking the time to understand your unique needs, goals, and habits, you can tailor a plan that is perfectly suited to your situation. This might involve combining elements of different methods, adjusting the specifics of a given method, or incorporating your own ideas and innovations. The goal is to create a plan that feels natural and comfortable for you, and that you are able to stick to over time.

It is important to keep in mind that your customized plan may evolve over time. As your needs and circumstances change, you may find that your plan needs to be adjusted. This is perfectly normal, and is part of the process of staying flexible and adapting as needed. By regularly re-evaluating your methods and making changes as needed, you can ensure that your customized plan continues to support your productivity and success.

However, it's also important to recognize that there are limits to what can be achieved in a day, and that there is such a thing as "good enough." By finding the right balance between productivity and relaxation, you can lead a more fulfilling life.

Staying flexible and adapting as needed is an important aspect of using productivity methods effectively. No single method is perfect for everyone, and what works best for one person may not work as well for another.

It is important to approach each method with an open mind and be willing to modify or adjust your approach as needed to suit your individual needs and preferences. This might involve experimenting with different methods, combining different approaches, or adjusting the specifics of a given method to suit your particular situation.

CHAPTER 13
TAKING YOUR FIRST STEPS

n this book, we've explored ten of the most popular productivity methods currently being used by individuals and businesses around the world. From the Pomodoro Technique, to the Eisenhower Matrix, to the Seinfeld Method, each of these methods offers a unique approach to increasing productivity and reducing stress.

One of the key takeaways from this book is that there is no one-size-fits-all approach to productivity. What works for one person might not work for another. That's why it's important to try out different methods and find what works best for you.

Another important aspect of productivity is work-life balance. Being more productive doesn't mean sacrificing your health or relationships. In fact, a well-implemented productivity method can actually free up more time to spend with loved ones and pursue hobbies and interests.

As you continue your journey towards increased productivity, it's important to stay flexible and adapt as needed.

Our lives and work are constantly changing, and our productivity methods should reflect that. Don't be afraid to make changes or try out new methods. The goal is to find what works best for you, and to continue to improve your productivity over time.

We hope this book has been helpful in providing you with the information and inspiration you need to get started on your own productivity journey. Whether you choose to implement one method, or a combination of methods, we wish you the best of luck as you work towards a more productive and fulfilling life. Take the first step towards a more productive and fulfilling life by starting to implement one of these productivity methods today!

FOR FURTHER READING

Here are some websites where you can find more information on the productivity methods discussed here:

POMODORO TECHNIQUE

- PomodoroTechnique.com
- LifeHacker.com/pomodoro-technique
- ForestApp.cc

GETTING THINGS DONE

- DavidCo.com (David Allen's official website)
- GTDConnect.com

TIME BLOCKING

- TimeBlocking.com
- Calendly.com/time-blocking
- ProductivityTheory.com/time-blocking

EISENHOWER MATRIX

- ProductivityTheory.com/eisenhower-matrix
- MindTools.com/pages/article/newHTE_08.htm
- TheProductivityPro.com/eisenhower-matrix

MIND MAPPING

- MindMapping.com
- MindNode.com
- TonyBuzan.com (official website of the creator of Mind Mapping)

KANBAN

- KanbanMethod.com
- Trello.com
- AgileAlliance.org/kanban

THE TWO MINUTE RULE

- gtdtimes.com/two-minute-rule/
- timemanagementninja.com/two-minute-rule/

THE 80/20 (PARETO) PRINCIPLE

- ProductivityTheory.com/pareto-principle
- TimeManagementNinja.com/pareto-principle
- Investopedia.com/terms/p/pareto-principle.asp

SEINFELD METHOD

- TheProductivityPro.com/seinfeld-method
- LifeHacker.com/the-seinfeld-productivity-secret
- Zestful.co/seinfeld-method

BATCH PROCESSING

- ProductivityTheory.com/batch-processing
- LifeHacker.com/batch-your-tasks-for-more-productivity
- Tim Ferriss' blog (Tim Ferriss is a proponent of batch processing)

These websites offer a wealth of information and resources on each of these productivity methods, including tips and techniques for implementation, tools and apps, and real-world examples of how others have used these methods to boost their productivity.

www.ingramcontent.com/pod-product-compliance
Lightning Source LLC
Chambersburg PA
CBHW070750220526
45467CB00018B/1840